CARMINA ARCHILOCHI

A thistle with graceful leaves.
MELEAGER The Garland

FOREWORD BY HUGH KENNER

CARMINA ARCHILOCHI
THE FRAGMENTS
OF ARCHILOCHOS

Translated from the Greek by GUY DAVENPORT

UNIVERSITY OF CALIFORNIA PRESS: *Berkeley and Los Angeles*
1964

UNIVERSITY OF CALIFORNIA PRESS
BERKELEY AND LOS ANGELES, CALIFORNIA
CAMBRIDGE UNIVERSITY PRESS
LONDON, ENGLAND

© 1964 BY THE REGENTS OF THE UNIVERSITY OF CALIFORNIA
LIBRARY OF CONGRESS CATALOG CARD NUMBER: 64-15135

For Lee Lescaze

FOREWORD

The *Iliad* of Homer, done into English verse (1715-1720) by Alexander Pope, may be said to depend, as a condition of its very existence, not only on Homer's text but on his substantial reputation. The mind of Pope's reader contains that reputation as surely as it contains the meaning of the word "elephant." The reputation, indeed, is one of Pope's balancing forces; it is entertaining to consider how strange a poem the English *Iliad* would seem had there been no Homer and had Mr. Pope, in eighteenth-century England, simply made it all up. Classical renderings are normally sheltered in this way; from the least deft translator of Homer or Aeschylus we will accept a rather large proportion of inelegance, in concession, we suppose, to the obduracies of his great original.

Mr. Davenport's work occupies a more exposed position, not incorporating the prestige of a literary monument. When sixteen of his fragments appeared in *Poetry* early in 1963, it was widely supposed that "Archilochos" was the invention of a new and ingenious American poet, a natural mistake in view of his exclusion from the Swinburnian Greece with which nonspecialists are still presented. This misunderstanding emphasizes the curious ability of these fragments to survive on their own, as poems in the American idiom, and suggests a good way to start reading them. Viewed in this context they are persuasively domestic, though they incorporate to be sure with magpie voracity some outlandish proper names and imply a military caste that fights with spears. This is, as the reader prefers, excellent fooling, or else a native poetic strategy: one recalls the "angwan-tíbo, potto, or loris" embedded in the poem by Marianne Moore which commences in the idiom of a Bell Telephone Company leaflet, or the resonant names of sages tesselated by Pound into Yankee homiletics. The arts in America have for fifty years been treating heterogeneous details as "found objects."

Now that we have the complete fragments in our hands, we can carry the game of misunderstanding a little further. Mr. Davenport would seem to have "invented" not only a poet and some poems, but a book: a fascinating thing of glimpses and tatters: lacunae, conjectures, maddening elisions. By a kind of inspired syncopation, the rip in the manuscript does not conveniently excise the bawdy word, but instead the words just after it. This verges on Dada; it is as though we had only what scholarship has been able to scrape together of a very ancient, unclassically recalcitrant poet, fitfully to be heard cursing his fate through layer upon shifting layer of obdurate silence.

To see the book in this way first of all is to reap the maximum enjoyment it can afford; for of course our next discovery will be that there was indeed a poet named Archilochos, and that he does exist solely in passages grammarians quoted to illustrate a point, or in fragments recoverable from mummies wrapped in the Alexandrian equivalent of old newspapers, so that we have no poem of his entire. And Mr. Davenport has been playing not the game of inventing a consistent body of lore, but the still more difficult game of sticking as close as possible to the actual Greek words unstuck from those mummies and now displayed with annotations of desperate diligence in the Budé edition of Messieurs Lasserre and Bonnard. This is, for our purposes, Archilochos; this is exactly how he exists, and how more of our classical heritage exists than we like to think; and we may as well savor the comedy of a situation there is no way of repairing. On two occasions a line, one likes to think of invective, has been eroded down to a single letter:

. . .n .

Sic semper poetis. The book in our hands has two authors, Archilochos and Guy Davenport, and a third coauthor, Chronos: devouring Time.

Sappho's text is in comparable shape, and her Loeb translator was at pains to "restore" it, papering over fissures with poetry of his own improvising. In the same way the "Victory from Samothrace" consists of one hundred and thirty pieces stuck together, with copious additions in plaster, including a plaster right wing but no plaster head: monument to a taste that preferred a counterfeit Hellas to the discrete pieces, but arrested its counterfeiting short of totality because the Elgin Marbles had taught it to cherish, if not bits, ruins. It is only very recently that a massive regrouping of our aesthetic decisions has enabled us, for perhaps the first time in the history of the West, to read bits without romanticizing our loss. The reader of Joyce or Pound perceives the detail not as a fragment from the whole but as a functioning component in the whole; the reader of Frobenius understands how a civilization goes down into its least details, each fraction eloquent; biologists study not entelechies but cells; we know how to look at a carburetor as a piece of sculpture. And this new understanding is in our time catching up with the always tardy art of translation.

That the past exists in the present just as it does, and not as we might like an imagination such as Walter Scott's to re-dream it, this is a lesson that translators have been slow in learning. They have asked themselves whether Homer was not a Greek Milton, or Euripides an Athenian Shakespeare, instead of staring very coldly at the actual texts of Homer or Euripides as these texts, lacunae, emendations and all, have actually been received. And classicists themselves are apt not to realize how much flabby invention is entailed in making Sappho sound like a she-Shelley, or Anacreon like a Regency tippler, or in finding Archilochos unfit to speak English at all. It is the standard translations that give us invented poets: invented minor poets on a par with Thomson and Collins. Translators were gazing at their sentimental chimerae long after scientists and poets had begun looking at pragmatic evidence. The age of creative literalness began when Pound rebuked the invention of a great predecessor ("Hang it all, Robert Browning") by citing what is actually discoverable about Sordello ("Lo Sordels si fo de Mantoana . . .").

Mr. Davenport's Archilochos, cursing despite scholarship's rags, is a contemporary poet, in a profound sense an invention. He has been made possible by our ability to engage the imagination with the pragmatic, by our renewed pleasure in the laconic and the expletive functions of language, and by our present willingness to assimilate these pleasures into our notion of Hellenism. He is also the product, so far as one can judge without having known Archilochos, of a personal affinity between translator and translated. And if he is "our" true Archilochos, he is like no Archilochos who has ever existed before. A story by Jorge Luis Borges invites us to imagine certain chapters of *Don Quixote* rewritten in the Spanish word for word by a twentieth-century Frenchman. This text, says Borges profoundly, is identical with that of Cervantes but "almost infinitely richer." The subtle relationship of Sr. Borges' fancy, translation at its best can almost realize, bringing forward the origins of a text long ruined, ruins and all, into another age. HUGH KENNER

TRANSLATOR'S NOTE

Archilochos is the second poet of the West. Before him the archpoet Homer had written the two poems of Europe; never again would one imagination find the power to move two epics to completion and perfection. The clear minds of these archaic, island-dwelling Greeks held a culture that we can know by a few details only, fragment by fragment, a temple, a statue of Apollo with a poem engraved down the thighs, generous vases with designs severely abstract and geometric. They decorated their houses and ships like Florentines and Japanese; they wrote poems like Englishmen of the court of Henry and Elizabeth and James. They dressed like Samurai; all was bronze, terra cotta, painted marble, dyed wool, and banquets. Of the Arcadian Greece of Winckelmann and Walter Pater they were as ignorant as we of the ebony cities of Yoruba and Benin. The scholar poets of the Renaissance, Ambrogio Poliziano and Christopher Marlowe, whose vision of antiquity we have inherited, would have rejected as indecorous this seventh-century world half oriental, half Viking. Archilochos was both poet and soldier, a mercenary. As a poet he was both satirist and lyricist. Iambic verse is his invention. He wrote the first beast fable known to us. He wrote marching songs, love lyrics of frail tenderness, elegies. But most of all he was what Meleager calls him, "a thistle with graceful leaves." There is a tradition that wasps hover around his grave. To the ancients, both Greek and Roman, he was The Satirist. And we have not a single whole poem of Archilochos.

We have what grammarians quote to illustrate a point of dialect or interesting use of the subjunctive; we have brief quotations from admiring critics; and we have papyrus fragments, scrap paper from the households of Alexandria, with which third-class mummies were wrapped and stuffed. All else is lost. Horace and Catullus, like all cultivated readers, had Archilochos complete in their libraries. What the living could not keep, the purposeless dead and the dullest of books have preserved.

Even in the tattered version we have of Archilochos, some three hundred fragments and about forty paraphrases and indirect quotations in the Budé edition (1958) of Professors Lasserre and Bonnard,* a good half of them beyond conjecture as to context, so ragged the papyrus, or brief ("grape," "curled wool," "short sword") the extraordinary form of his mind is discernible. Not all poets can be so broken and still compel attention.

Like the brutal but gallant *Landsknecht* Urs Graf, both artist and soldier, or the *condottiere,* poet, military engineer, and courtly amorist Sigismondo Malatesta of Rimini, Archilochos kept his "two services" in an unlikely harmony. Ares did not complain that this ashspear fighter wrote poems, and

* Archiloque, *Fragments,* texte établi par François Lasserre, traduit et commenté par André Bonnard, Collection des Universités de France, publiée sous le patronage de l'Association Guillaume Budé, Paris, 1958.

the Muses have heard everything and did not mind that their horse-tail-helmeted servant sometimes spoke with the vocabulary of a paratrooper sergeant, though the high-minded Spartans banned Archilochos' poems for their obscenity. And the people of his native Paros made it clear, when they honored him with a public monument, that they thought him a great poet in spite of his nettle tongue and his propensity to enpurple the air.

Apollo read Archilochos with delight and was of the opinion that his poems would last as long as mankind. "Hasten on, Wayfarer," Archilochos' tomb bore for inscription, "lest thou stir up the hornets." Leonidas the epigrammatist imagined the Muses hopelessly in love with Archilochos, and Delian Apollo to boot, for how else account for such melody, such verve? Quintilian admired his richness of blood, meaning liveliness, one supposes, and his abundance of muscle. Plutarch in his essay on music places Archilochos among the innovators of metric, and Horace, imitating Archilochos, congratulated himself on bringing Greek numbers into Italy. Stern Pindar called him Archilochos the Scold. Writers as different as Milton, who mentions him in the *Areopagitica* as trying the patience of the defenders of the freedom of speech, and Wyndham Lewis, who spits like a cat at his reputation, took his satiric talent for granted without really knowing what he wrote. Hipponax alone among the archaic poets, we are told, had as sharpened a stylus as Archilochos, and Hipponax is remembered for a black little distich:

> Woman is twice a pleasure to man,
> The wedding night and her funeral.

Though he is said to have written with venom, and, according to Gaitylikos, splashed Helicon with gore, we have no evidence of anything so caustic. We have to take antiquity's word for it, or assume that the Panhellenes were far touchier than we about satire. Certainly their sense of honor was of an iron strictness. To mock, a Greek proverb goes, is to thumb through Archilochos. "The longer your letters, the better," Aristophanes complimented a friend, "like the poems of Archilochos."

Of the man himself we know that he was born on Paros in the Cyclades seven centuries before Christ. Pausanius knew a tradition that makes him the descendant of one Tellis, or Telesicles, who was distinguished enough to have figured in Polygnotos' frescoes at Delphi, where he is shown with Kleoboia, who introduced the Eleusinian mysteries into Thasos, an island that owes much to Archilochos' family. A Byzantine encyclopedia credits his father with founding a town in Thasos, "an island crowned with forests and lying in the sea like the backbone of an ass," as he describes it in a poem. And Arichilochos himself seems to have lived in Thasos at one time.

Since his name means First Sergeant (leader of a company of ash-spearmen or hoplites), he may have given it to himself, or used it as a *nom de guerre et de plume*. Some scholars guess that he was illegitimate, accepted by his father but the son of a slave woman named Enipo. The poems reveal a man who took pride in his hard profession of mercenary, who cultivated a studied lyric eroticism, and had a tender fancy for landscape. His companion was one Glaukos, Grey Eyes, and several fragments address him in a fatherly manner. At one time he contracted marriage with a daughter of Lykambes, Neobulé, probably a settlement that would retire him from campaigning. "O to touch Neobulé's hand!" is the oldest surviving fragment of a love lyric in Greek. But Lykambes took back his word and the wedding was canceled. All Greece soon knew, and later, Rome, Archilochos' bitter poem in which he wished that Lykambes might freeze, starve, and be frightened to death simultaneously. And all schoolboys, before Greek was expelled from classrooms, knew Lykambes to be synonymous with a broken word of honor.

Archilochos was killed by a man named Crow. The death was either in battle or a fair fight; nevertheless, Apollo in grief and anger excommunicated Crow from all the temples; so spoke the entranced oracle at Delphi.

Sappho's "I loved you once, Atthis, and long ago," Swift's "Only a woman's hair," are sharp in brevity. The rest of Sappho's poem is mildew and papyrus dust. Swift could write no more. Fragments, when they are but motes (the unfinished works of a Spenser or a Michelangelo are a different matter), touch us as the baby glove of a pharoah that moved William Carlos Williams to tears, or the lock of Lucrezia Borgia's hair that drew Byron back day after day to gaze (and to steal one strand for Landor); they "brave time" with a mite's grip, missing by a rotten piece of linen or a grammarian's inadvertent immortality the empty fame of the sirens' song. To exist in fragments and in Greek is a doubly perilous claim on the attention of our time.

The two hundred and eighty-seven fragments here translated into verse represent all that could be made to answer to English sense, and in some extremely torn ones I have relied on the conjectures of Professor Lasserre. In one instance I have translated a fragment in its original isolation and as the possible beginning of another fragment, which Lasserre takes to be its continuation. I have been as literal as an amateur's Greek can manage. When fourteen of these fragments, in an earlier version, appeared in *Poetry*, I found that it was assumed by readers that the translation was "very free." It is not, or, Archaic Greek being difficult, is not meant to be. Another assumed that I had invented Archilochos. Such is the ignorance of a great poet, however much in ruin, which I hope this translation can help to correct.

I have not tried to do anything with the lines that appear

on the "large block of Parian marble preserved in the museum at Paroikia," split, erased, chipped, and hacked at, and in editions of Archilochos largely within brackets.

After the first version of this translation fell into the publisher's hands, Professor Keith Aldrich undertook to compare translation with original, sometimes to his dismay, to point out variant readings among editors of Archilochos, and to distinguish sure fragments from dubious ones. For this backtracking and scrutiny and its attendant criticism I am thankful, not only for the painstaking technical advice but also for the patience and sympathy with which it was recorded for my benefit. Professor Aldrich also suggested that I need not omit a fragment because it was trivial away from its context; where everything is a glittering heap of scraps it seems wrong to include

> Let us hide the sea-king's gifts,
> The wrecked dead Poseidon brings.

and to omit

"on to Thasos."

But I must insist that the translation still contains readings about which Professor Aldrich has his doubts and he is not to share the ignominy of cackle and objection which the critics are perfectly justified in leveling at some of my ignorances. Classrooms are magic places, with their Geometric Period Mimnermus diagrammed in chalk on the blackboard, and the learned Minoru Hara to one's left, thinking in Japanese, yet the impulse to translate Archilochos comes as much from the barracks of the XVIII Airborne Corps and of the 756th Heavy Artillery, and I know not what tone Robert Gallway's Matchless added to Version I or Steven Diamant's Norton and Seefab javelin to Version II, but the clarity and irony of Mary Ann Mott's imagination I know well and acknowledge strenuously.

To Cedric Whitman and Hugh Kenner this translation owes its existence, for without their encouragement I would not have undertaken the job at all. And fortune has been good about joining my walks around Haverford with those of the scholar Arnold Post, so that we could talk Archilochos under dogwood and oak.

GUY DAVENPORT

Haverford College, 1963

CONTENTS

Foreword by Hugh Kenner   *vii*

Translator's Note   *xiii*

THE FRAGMENTS   3

Concordance and Notes   98

THE FRAGMENTS

1

Sergeant to Enyalios,
The great god War,
I practise double labor.
With poetry, that lover's gift,
I serve the lady Muses.

2

My ash spear is my barley bread,
My ash spear is my Ismarian wine.
I lean on my spear and drink.

3

Let him go ahead.
Ares is a democrat.
There are no privileged people
On a battlefield.

4

This island,
>   garlanded with wild woods,
Lies in the sea
>   like the backbone of an ass.

5

>   Listen to me cuss.

6

>   Pallas Athena and our strong arms,
>   That victory. From hill to hill in retreat
>   We walked backward under their javelins
>   Until we reached the rampart of stones
>   She, Zeus' daughter, led us toward.
>   We attacked later, chanting hymns
>   Of Mytilenian Apollo, while they,
>   Keeping their courage with harp and song,
>   Fell back to their hill, withered by arrows.
>   We crossed a harvest of our dead.

7

[*A rag of paper,
but*]

Bright clean air.
For you are

A brave man
And honorable.

Wandering
Aimlessness
Of evil.

8

What hair styles among
All this jackass backsided
Sabazian pederasty.

9

With ankles that fat
It must be a girl.

10

When the fight's with those hard Euboians,
No bow-strings' whine or snap of bow-notch
Or whip of sling do you hear, but a delirium
Of Ares, sword work and spear sticking,
The tall Euboians famous for their knives.

11

Like Odysseus under the ram
You have clung under your lovers
And under your love of lust,
Seeing nothing else for this mist,
Dark of heart, dark of mind.

12

As a dove to a sheaf of wheat,
So friends to you.

13

His mane the infantry
Cropped down to stubble.

14

These golden matters
Of Gyges and his treasuries
Are no concern of mine.
Jealousy has no power over me,
Nor do I envy a god his work,
And I don't burn to rule.
Such things have no
Fascination for my eyes.

15

[*Shredded paper, but*]
Whittles
      to carry
[*here teething moths
have passed*]
      I repulse
Your great kindness
[*holes*]
Kindness.

16

Shield against shield,
Keep the shield-wall tight.
And the gift of death
They bring, let no man take.

17

She held
      a sprig of myrtle she'd picked
And a rose
That pleased her most
Of those on the bush
And her long hair shaded
      her shoulders and back.

18

      The young with blue javelins
      For the games, young leaves
      In coronets over young ears,
      Have yet to see battle spears
      Thick as chaff in the air.

19

Poseidon rider of horses
Has spared the captain
Of our fifty men.

20

Decks awash,
Mast-top dipping,
And all
Balanced on the keen edge
Now of the wind's sword,
Now of the wave's blade.

21

Dazzling radiance.

22

Pass by,
Highborn sir.

23

Attribute all to the gods.
They pick a man up,
Stretched on the black loam,
And set him on his two feet,
Firm, and then again
Shake solid men until
They fall backward
Into the worst of luck,
Wandering hungry,
Wild of mind.

24

The oxherd picks tarantulas from his oxen,
The cocksman keeps his prick dainty and clean:
The nature of man is surprising and diverse,
Each finding his pleasure where the heart wills,
And each can say, I alone among mankind
Have what's best, what's fine and good
From Zeus, God, Father of men and gods.
Yet Eurymas finds fault with everybody.

25

[   ]
Slime and crud
[   ]
Snot

26

[*The left side
Of a poem:*]

Nasty
Which thinks
Woman
Hatefullest
And father
Dear
Not O
Upon

27

Remember us, remember this earth,
When with hearts against despair
Our javelins held Thasos from her enemy.

28

Dripping blood.

29

Miserable with desire
I lie lifeless,
My bones shot through
With thorny anguish
Sent by the gods.

30

She's as timid
As a partridge.

31

Hear me here,
Hugging your knees,
Hephaistos Lord.
My battle mate,
My good luck be;
That famous grace
Be my grace too.

32

Whoever is alive
Is pleased by song.

33

Stirred up and raving.

34

You are too old
For perfume.

35

And the heart
Is pleased
By one thing
After another.

36

He comes, in bed,
As copiously as
A Prienian ass
And is equipped
Like a stallion.

37

Their duenna in their midst,
Those girls
    wore such perfume
In their hair
    and on their breasts
Even old men
Desired them.
    And, Glaukos my boy,
Their cunts
[*but here the papyrus is torn*]

A parade of girls
From that shuttered house
With all its coming
And going.
What shoes!
[*here the papyrus is too tattered to read*]

Ignorance
Of the good
Of things.

38

You bring home
A bright evil.

39

But iron bends,
Too, and that poker
Is limp as a rag
Most of the time.

40

Friends hurt
The most.

41

A few citizens
Hung back,
But the majority.

42

There are other shields to be had,
But not under the spear-hail
Of an artillery attack,
In the hot work of slaughtering,
Among the dry racket of the javelins,
Neither seeing nor hearing.

43

Be bold! That's one way
Of getting through life.
So I turn upon her
And point out that,
Faced with the wickedness
Of things, she does not shiver.
I prefer to have, after all,
Only what pleases me.
Are you so deep in misery
That you think me fallen?

You say I'm lazy; I'm not,
Nor any of my kin-people.
I know how to love those
Who love me, how to hate.
My enemies I overwhelm
With abuse. The ant bites!
The oracle said to me:
"Return to the city, reconquer.
It is almost in ruins.
With your spear give it glory.
Reign with absolute power,
The admiration of men.
After this long voyage,
Return to us from Gortyne."
Pasture, fish, nor vulture
Were you, and I, returned,
Seek an honest woman
Ready to be a good wife.
I would hold your hand,
Would be near you, would have run
All the way to your house.
I cannot. The ship went down,
And all my wealth with it.
The salvagers have no hope.
You whom the soldiers beat,
You who are all but dead,
How the gods love you!
And I, alone in the dark,
I was promised the light.

44

Courtyard barricaded by a wall.

45

You led us
A thousand strong
At Thasos.

46

Athena daughter of thundering Zeus
Brings them courage in their battles,
That weeping people, every man of them a woman.
Whereupon, the sun of grace upon them,
They build new houses and clean new fields.
They have retreated, as if by habit,
From land after land, without arousing
The least pity in any possible defender.
Now by the will of all the gods on Olympos,
This island.

47

A coat of wool
That seems woven
Of piddock shell
And dyed purple.

48

Golden hair.

49

[This shred
Of Alexandrian
Paper, torn
Left side, right side,
Top and bottom,
With moth-holes
In the middle,
Reads]

    You
       if
    river
       so
    around
    I, then, alone

50

Watch, Glaukos, Watch!
Heavy and high buckles the sea.
A cloud tall and straight
Has gathered on the Gyrean mountain-tops,
Forewarning of thunder, lightning, wind.
What we don't expect comes fearfully.
War, Glaukos, war.

51

Yes, yes,
As sure as a poppy's
Green.

52

Zeus is the best priest among the gods;
He himself fulfills what he prophesies.

53

Fields fattened
By corpses.

54

The arrogant
Puke pride.

55

Until,
And,
Mountain tops.

56

Field rations,
Legitimacy,
Heart.

57

Hot tears cannot drive misery away,
Nor banquets and dancing make it worse.

58

From Paros
The lovely
We march.

59

Phasinos,
        dawn shows,
And now it is the Thargelia.

60

But for what he did
To me,
He won't get away
Unstruck.

61

Ass kisser!

62

The highly polished minds
Of accomplished frauds.

63

You've bolted
The door.

64

[   ]
    you are busy with
of Imbros
      repulses
    well-wishing
and I hope
    making use of
      busy
to drive into confusion
        having
  [   ]

65

There is a fable among men:
How a fox and an eagle
Joined in partnership.
[*three decipherable fragments survive:*]
EAGLE:　See that high crag there?
　　　　　The rough one,
　　　　　　　　the forbidding one?

To get up there you climb
With nimble wings,
Flying from the earth to
The high rock,
Lifting up thus.

O Zeus, Father Zeus,
　　　　yours is heaven's strength,
And you see the works of men,
　　　　both villainous and law-abiding.
To you the uprightness and sinning pride
Of the animals are significant.

66

A sharp helmsman
And a brave heart
With a two-master.

67

Thief and the night,
Thief and the night.

68

I think
[   ]
Know then
    that I am so minded
[   ]
To suffer.

69

Foggy island.

70

What breaks me,
Young friend,
Is tasteless desire,
Dead iambics,
Boring dinners.

71

Greet insolence with outrage.

72

Soul, soul,
Torn by perplexity,
On your feet now!
Throw forward your chest
To the enemy;
Keep close in the attack;
Move back not an inch.
But never crow in victory,
Nor mope hang-dog in loss.
Overdo neither sorrow nor joy:
A measured motion governs man.

73

The old men are idle,
And should be,
Especially when
Simplicity and stubbornness
Blunder and prate.

74

Little boy.

75

Medlar trees.

76

To make you laugh,
Charilaos Erasmonides
And best of my friends,
Here's a funny story.

77

The son of
The fig eater.

78

Moral blindness
Miserable
    worthless
Jealousy
    O heart
and not

79

Some Saian mountaineer
Struts today with my shield.
I threw it down by a bush and ran
When the fighting got hot.
Life seemed somehow more precious.
It was a beautiful shield.
I know where I can buy another
Exactly like it, just as round.

80

Twice the age of her apprentices,
That wrinkled old madam Xanthé
Is still regarded as an expert.

81

Her hair was as simple
As flax, and I,
I am heavy with infamy.

82

Desire,
Future,
Enemy.
Music:
My song
And a flute
Together.

83

Keep a mercenary for a friend
Glaukos, to stand by in battle.

84

Touched girl.

85

That old goat
Patrolled his own corridors.

86

Everything,
Perikles,
A man has
Destiny and
Chance
Gave him.

87

Everything
People have
Comes from
Painstaking
Work.

88

Recompense.

89

Plums.

90

[*Paper
Snowflake:*]

Dwells here
      hard fate
participate

91

      When Alkibié married,
      She made of her copious hair
      A holy gift to Hera.

92

There is no land like this,
So longable for, so pretty,
So enjoyable,
Here on the banks of the Siris.

93

The heart of mortal man,
Glaukos, son of Leptines,
Is what Zeus makes it,
Day after day,
And what the world makes it,
That passes before our eyes.

94

                The cave,
And henceforth I intend to
Conduct my life with more order
[*here the papyrus deteriorates*]
        Line, dog, solitude.
[*the papyrus gets worse*]
What can I offer in exchange?
[*and worse*]
Against the night-prowler
Mount guard around your house.
I have seen him in the streets,
Plotting burglaries.

95

[   ]
[   ]
Think
[   ]
[   ]
[   ]
[   ]
   happy

96

To engage with an insatiable girl,
Ramming belly against belly,
Thigh riding against thigh.

97

Zeus gave them
A dry spell.

98

Long the time, hard the work
That went into heaping the wealth
He threw away awhoring.

99

[   ]
[   ]
(ulcer?)

100

Naked.

101

With ships so trim and narrow,
Ropes fast and sails full,
I ask of the gods that
Our comrades have a wind too,
That they meet neither tall wave
Nor reef.
      All fortune be with them.

102

Tenella Kallinike!
　Hail Lord Herakles!
You and Iolas, soldiers two,
Tenella Kallinike!
　Hail Lord Herakles!

103

Wild animals.

104

Our very meeting
With each other
Is an omen.

105

Has no liver,
But, even so,
Hot as a hornet.

106

[*A thin
Ribbon of
Paper*]

Wine
[   ]
Concerns
[   ]
Weeps
[   ]
Inclines
[   ]
Crash

107

Begotten by
Their father's
Roaring farts.

108

His attachment to the despicable
Is so affectionate and stubborn,
Argument can't reach him.

109

Battle trumpet.

110

A man, Aisimedes, who listens
To what people say about him
Isn't ever going to be quiet of mind.

111

Lying down
In the olive press.

112

A ditch all around,
        wild animals,
           and speed,
His inheritance from his father
That girl tried
            cooked goose
Eaten.

113

There's nothing now
We can't expect to happen!
Anything at all, you can bet,
Is ready to jump out at us.
No need to wonder over it.
Father Zeus has turned
Noon to night, blotting out
The sunshine utterly,
Putting cold terror
At the back of the throat.
Let's believe all we hear.
Even that dolphins and cows
Change place, porpoises and goats,
Rams booming along in the offing,
Mackerel nibbling in the hill pastures.
I wouldn't be surprised,
I wouldn't be surprised.

114

Venom of a water-snake.

115

Gently cock
The trap's spring

116

Let us sing,
Ahem,
Of Glaukos who wore
The pompadour.

117

Damp
Crotch.

118

Where, where,
O Erxias,
Is the guidon stuck
Of this company
With its luck shot?

119

    Otherwise,
           that stone of Tantalos
    Will hang over this island.

120

    Not a rampart held.

121

Grief and fasting in anguish
Strike city street and dinner table.
We complain, we dream, we blame.
This sea-cyclone calamity,
This storm-wave pounding our hearts
—with hiss and thunder together
It climbed to knock flat
With an orchard of foam on top—
Has mauled us and choked us with hurt.
What are backbones if not ramrods?
The gods toughen us, Perikles,
To stand this pain. Fortune, misfortune;
Misfortune, fortune. Grit your teeth.
Not all of us need be women.

122

Night.
The wind
Blows landward.
Branches
Creak.

123

He made all secure against
High seas and wind.

124

Justice.

125

[   ] take
[   ] heart and what
You have [   ]

126

Thasos,
Calamitous city.

127

O Hephaistos Lord of Fire,
How awful to be your suppliant!

128

Put down the uproar.

129

    Why should the sea be fat
    With my drowned friends?
    Why oil the knees of the gods?
    Why, why should Hephaistos
    The Fire dance his dance
    And feast on these runner's legs
    Poseidon the Water has stilled?
    To the ecstatic fire we give to eat
    This fine body wrapped in white,
    Pleasure once of glad women,
    Companion once of Ares, War.

130

  Every man
  Stripped naked.

131

Of holy Demeter
And of her daughter
The festival attending.

132

Mountain animal.

133

When the people went off to the Games,
Batousiades came along too.

134

Great virtue
In the feet.

135

And close to me.

136

The good-natured need no cutlery
In their vocabulary.

137

worst,
[   ]
Lykambes

138

Elegant frog.

139

A great squire he was,
And heavy with a stick
In the sheeplands of Asia.

140

Rigidities melt;
Masts fall.

141

O forsaken and hungry
People of the city,
Hear me speak.

142

And no man thereafter
With the gods.

143

Hang iambics.
This is no time
For poetry.

144

Fortune is like a wife:
Fire in her right hand,
Water in her left.

145

Swift of foot.

146

Like the men
Of Thrace or Phrygia
She could get her wine down
At a go,
Without taking a breath,
While the flute
Played a certain little tune,
And like those foreigners
She permitted herself
To be buggared.

147

Upon the roads
Of Ennyra.

148

But, to you, this new thing
[   ]
weigh in the balance
[   ]
Pleas[ure]

149

The seam of
The scrotum.

          150

          Into the jug
          Through a straw.

151

Sparks in wheat.

          152

          [   ]
          Kerykides his
          [   ]
          quiv[er]

153

You drink a lot of unmixed wine
That you haven't paid for,
And weren't invited to share,
Treating everybody as your dearest friend,
Greed having supplanted any shame
You once had.

154

[*The right-hand
Line endings
Of an elegy:*]

moves against;
staunching,

sharp-pointed penis,
I, as usual,
situate;
suffice.
the city,
therefore you imagine,
we establish beauty.

155

Eaten by fleas.

156

She sweetened
Her voice.

157

He turned.

158

Sabazians
Of the
Elegant
Hair.

159

Of the sons of Selles.

160

Humpbacked
Everytime he can.

161

Deer-heart.

162

He's yoke-broke
But shirks work,
Part bull, part fox,
My sly ox.

163

Idle chatter.

164

This, this
We cannot do.

165

Illusionist in language
And pretentious buffoon.

166

The crow was so ravished by pleasure
That the kingfisher on a rock nearby
Shook its feathers and flew away.

167

There the thrones
Of great Zeus
And his rocks
For throwing.

168

Seven of the enemy
        were cut down in that encounter
And a thousand of us,
        mark you,
Ran them through.

169

They'll say I was a mercenary,
Like a Carian. Such was life.
Don't call the medics over,
I know a way, not theirs,
To get a swelling like that down.
Listen here, now. No? Forget it.
They'll say I was a mercenary.
Is there clean linen for a shroud?

170

One sizable thing I do know:
How to get back my own
With a man doing me wrong.

171

Ignorant and ill bred
Mock the dead.

172

With what springs
In my legs
I leapt the rocks.

173

Keep a quiet heart.
We move into battle.
Come down among us,
    O Zeus!
The ground is our blood.
Long ships in the bay.

174

Their lives
Held in the arms
Of the waves.

175

Erxias, Defender, how can we muster
Our scattered troops? The campfires
Lift their smoke around the city.
The enemy's sharp arrows grow
Like bristles on our ships. The dead
Parch in the sun. The charges are bolder,
Knifing deep into the Naxos lines.
We scythe them down like tall grass
But they hardly feel our attacks.
The people will believe that we accept
With indifference these locust men
Who stamp our parents' fields to waste.
My heart must speak, for fear
And grief keep my neighbors silent.
Listen, hear me. Help comes from Thasos,
Too long held back by Toronaios;
And from Paros in the fast ships.
The captains are furious, and rage
To attack as soon as the auxiliaries
Are here. Smoke hangs over the city.
Send us men, Erxias. The auguries
Are good. I know you will come.

176

Truth is born
As lightning strikes.

177

       Against the wall, fists on hips,
       They leaned in a fish-net of shadow.

178

Sword
[   ]
was placed.

179

       Scallop.

180

Wood carved
To curve.

181

      feet
[swear!]
[   ]

182

With Aphrodita
Audacity wilts.

183

Fox knows many,
Hedgehog one
Solid trick.

Aliter,
Fox knows
Eleventythree
Tricks and still
Gets caught;
Hedgehog knows
One but it
Always works.

184

In the hospitality of war
We left them their dead
As a gift to remember us by.

185

[   ]
from what
[   ]

186

I hold out my hand
And beg.

187

I weep that the people of Thasos
Are in trouble;
The Magnesians
Are not my concern.

188

      Beautiful
                     consider
          and

189

Teaches the law
Of Crete.

190

    And may the dog days
    Blister the lot.

191

Kindly pass the cup down the deck
And keep it coming from the barrel,
Good red wine, and don't stir up the dregs,
And don't think why we shouldn't be,
More than any other, drunk on guard duty.

192

Charon the carpenter,
Citizen of Thasos.

193

The Cretan.

194

   my
Wander
  just as

195

What a burden off my neck!
What a joy to escape marriage!
Another time, Lykambes,
    father-in-law almost.
I can't bring you to your knees.
Honor presupposes a sense of shame,
And that you haven't got.

196

[*A scrap
Of paper:*]

Slavery,
Not for me,
But then.

197

Here's a fable, O Kerykides,
With a cudgel for a moral.
A monkey was no longer welcome
In animal society,
And went away, all alone.
Whereupon the fox, his mind
Thick with mischief and plots,
Began hatching a little scheme.

———

Water in one hand, fire in the other,
Cursing the fate of overseers, servants.

———

The Carpathian, the martyr

———

Just ahead, there was the trap

———

And a cage of iron

198

[   ]
[   ]
How?
[   ]
[   ]
  to
paying,
[   ]

199

Myself the choir-master
In the chant to Apollo,
Sung to the flute in Lesbos.

200

Tall Megatimos,
High Aristophon,
Pillars of Naxos,
O Great World,
You hold upright.

201

Grape.

202

With head thrown back and long throat,
Crying *Euaí*! in the Bacchanalia.
                      strong heart
[   ]
    of curious craft
Having remained
        [   ]
        houses

203

He went away, leaving behind a band of seven
To get Peisistratos' son home, men who
Kept order easily with zither and fife.
He had led them into Thasos to steal back
The tribute gold from the raging Thracians:
Great success, for them, for which the people
Paid with grief.

204

From dawn onwards
Each drank.
It was the feast of Bacchus.

205

As one fig tree in a rocky place
Feeds a lot of crows,
Easy-going Pasiphilé
Receives a lot of strangers.

206

They chased him
Down the mountain.

207

One half,
One third.

208

Utterly unrefined.

209

A hummock
Of a bulge
At the crotch,
That diner
On eyeless eels.

210

Mega [   ]
    slavery
Ex [   ]
  [   ]

211

There goes that
Cornet player.

212

There's no man she hasn't
Skinned alive.

213

Now that Leophilos is the governor,
Leophilos meddles in everybody's business,
And everybody falls down before Leophilos,
And all you hear is Leophilos, Leophilos.

214

  tree t[runk]
and comp[anion]
      jawbone
[   ]

215

Fortune save us from
These hairy-bottomed fellows.

216

Tender horn.

217

How did you become *so* bald,
Not a hair on your nape, even?

218

Fight!
I want a fight
With you
As a thirsty man
Wants water.

219

What a behind,
O monkey!

220

Impostor.

221

Lykambes' daughter
To the furthermost village.

222

In copulating
One discovers
That.

223

[   ]
He replied.

224

Season follows season,
Time grows old.

225

Old and
At home.

226

It's not your enemies
But your friends
You've got to watch.

227

I knocked him out the door
With a vine-stump cudgel.

228

[wa]x-soft.

229

Servant to
The Muses.

230

[   ] wor[k]
toward Thasos
[   ]

231

No man dead
Feels his fellows' praise.
We strive instead,
Alive, for the living's honor,
And the neglected dead
Can neither honor
Nor glory in praise.

232

O that
I might but touch
Neobulé's hand.

233

Nightingale.

234

Curl hung
In curl.

235

Paros,
      figs,
           life of the sea,
Fare thee well!

236

Soon [   ]
[   ] dogs

237

The lion ripped him open,
Poor fellow, as soon as
He entered the cave,
And dined on his tripes.

238

Let us hide the sea-king's gifts,
The wrecked dead Poseidon brings.

239

Swordsman and murderous son
Of the blood-drinker Ares.

240

    arou[nd]
    toward Thasos
[   ] accomplishment

241

Biting sword.

242

Courage comes with the man
Or he's no soldier of mine.

243

Lips covered with foam.

244

How it has all crashed together,
Panhellenic disaster,
            here on Thasos!

245

From there.

246

Women eager
To recline.

247

Jackass
Hot to mate.

248

Unicorn.

249

And I know how to lead off
The sprightly dance
Of the Lord Dionysos,
          the dithyramb.
I do it thunderstruck
With wine.

250

Arthmiades,
This present take,
Wine jugs and wine.
A man of glory,
Precise with power,
Wherever among men,
Your might strikes,
Astonishment grips
Who sees.

251

Retreat, confusion,
That army.
They were strong.
Hermes saved me.

252

Apollo our protector,
Slay the wicked.

253

You can't even cross a river
Without having to pay a toll.

254

Lyk[ambes?]
[   ]
wi[th]

255

Sons scythed down
By the governor.

256

The child of
Married people.

257

Soothing.

258

In jeopardy
On two horns

259

[ho(w?)   ]
[up from beneath?]

260

Papa Lykambes,
What's this you've thought up?
What's distracted the mind
You once had?
Mind? You're a laugh.

261

You've gone back on your word
Given over salt and table.

262

May he lose his way on the cold sea
And swim to the heathen Salmydessos,
May the ungodly Thracians with their hair
Done up in a fright on the top of their heads
Grab him, that he know what it is to be alone
Without friend or family. May he eat slave's bread
And suffer the plague and freeze naked,
Laced about with the nasty trash of the sea.
May his teeth knock the top on the bottom
As he lies on his face, spitting brine,
At the edge of the cold sea, like a dog.
And all this it would be a privilege to watch,
Giving me great satisfaction as it would,
For he took back the word he gave in honor,
Over the salt and table at a friendly meal.

263

Are you not willing to be whipped
Now that you've broken your promise?

264

I consider nothing
That's evil.

265

Father Zeus,
I've had
No wedding feast.

266

I've worn out
My dick.

267

Desire the limb-loosener,
O my companion,
Has beat me down.

268

Voracious, even,
To the bounds
Of cannibalism.

269

I overreached
And another
Bears the bother.

270

What demon tracks you down,
What anger behind this terror?

271

Against
[   ]
In the heart.

272

Strong lords
Of Naxos.

273

No more
Your face blooms
Soft. Lovely,
It withers.

274

Overlook my ways.
I'm countrified.

275

She's fat, public,
And a whore.

276

Uninspired but sentimental
Over one sadness or another
As a subject for his poems,
The voluble poet whets his stylus.

277

Curled wool.

278

In time of shame,
Can you spare me the evil?
Kindness flows both ways.
Woman, woman,
Why do you keep me here,
Why this road, of all,
And why do you care at all?

279

How many times,
How many times,
On the grey sea,
The sea combed
By the wind
Like a wilderness
Of woman's hair,
Have we longed,
Lost in nostalgia,
For the sweetness
Of homecoming.

280

So thick the confusion,
Even the cowards were brave.

281

Birdnests
In myrtle.

282

I do despise a tall general,
One of those swaggerers,
A curly-haired, cheek-frilled
Whisker dandy.

For me a proper officer's
Short and bow-legged,
Both feet planted well apart,
Tough in the guts.

283

Give the spear-shy young
Courage.
Make them learn
The battle's won
By the gods.

284

Raise your arms
To Demeter.

285

Now your apron-strings won't tie,
We know your ways.
Hipponax knows them better than any,
And Ariphantos,
Who was spared smelling the thief
Stinking of the goat he'd stolen,
By being away at the wars.

286

Well, my
Prong's unreliable,
And has just about
Stood his last.

287

When you upbraid me
For my poems,
Catch also a cricket
By the wings,
And shout at him
For chirping.

CONCORDANCE AND NOTES

The numbers in brackets refer to the text of Archilochos established by François Lasserre, published in 1958 by the Association Guillaume Budé: *Archiloque, Fragments, texte établi par François Lasserre, traduit et commenté par André Bonnard*, Paris. Since I first read Archilochos in J. M. Edmonds' *Elegy and Iambus*, Vol. II, Harvard University Press, 1931 (reprinted 1954), the scholar will find slight traces of that edition in my translation, and twice I have preferred Edmonds' reading to Lasserre's.

1. [8] Possibly a complete poem.
2. [7]
3. [111]
4. [17] The island is Thasos, where Archilochos' father founded a settlement.
5. [179]
6. [110] A badly mangled fragment, restored by conjecture.
7. [65] A mere shred of papyrus.

8. [181-183] Three discrete fragments joined this way on the evidence of an underground temple to Cotytto frequented by Sabazian homosexuals. Archilochos' acid remarks about hairstyles turn up in several other fragments.
9. [186]
10. [9]
11. [245]
12. [Edmonds 105]
13. [26] Long hair was a haz-

98

ard in close fighting, as the enemy could grab it if matters came to that.

14. [15] For the opulence of Gyges, see Herodotus.

15. [60] Shredded papyrus strip.

16. [114] Death as a gift: a prophylactic use of language common in Archilochos.

17. [40] A sense of tender beauty akin to that of the Pompeian painters.

18. [77 + 273] Improvisation based on two fragments about the recruit's skill with the javelin, *hommage à le javelot Seefab Sandviken* and its Eakins blue.

19. [243]

20. [Edmonds 43] The first two lines are supplied, to give substance to the metaphor.

21. [75] Papyrus fragment.

22. [195]

23. [123]

24. [36] Badly mangled text.

25. [76] Papyrus fragment.

26. [39] The left quarter or fifth of a poem torn vertically.

27. [107] Largely conjecture and restoration.

28. [191] Bonnard gives "ear dripping blood."

29. [266] This sounds like Courtly Love. It is rather raw sexual desire.

30. [192]

31. [86]

32. [262]

33. [151]

34. [237]

35. [Edmonds 36]

36. [184]

37. [38] Seriously torn and for the most part illegible.

38. [257]

39. [247]

40. [119]

41. [155]

42. [113] Losing his shield seemed to be the peculiar bad luck of Archilochos.

43. [35] Very badly torn.

44. [31]

45. [108]

46. [101]

47. [290]

48. [297]

49. [55]

50. [103] Since Demeas of Paros has explained that the imagery of the gathering storm is from a poem about the beginning of a war, I have supplied "War, Glaukos, war!" as a final line to the fragment.

51. [196]

52. [223]

53. [301] From a paraphrase.

54. [274] More literally, and more mysterious, "Having hanged themselves, they vomited their mass of pride."

55. [59] Badly torn fragment.

56. [57] Mere scrap of paper.

57. [5]

58. [136] The middle of three lines only.

59. [305]

Concordance and Notes 99

60. [176]
61. [248]
62. [252]
63. [254]
64. [137] A strip of paper with line-endings only.
65. [168-171]
66. [33]
67. [20] Badly torn fragment.
68. [138] Badly torn fragment.
69. [263]
70. [249]
71. [133] Torn on both sides.
72. [118]
73. [334] Only the first line is Archilochos'; the rest is probably an imitation (Lasserre).
74. [319]
75. [153] Bonnard translates Erasmonides as "son of love."
76. [214]
77. [158]
78. [77] Fragment torn on both edges.
79. [13]
80. [204-205]
81. [256] "and I, I" is a conjecture of Lasserre's.
82. [44] Badly torn fragment.
83. [6]
84. [323]
85. [222]
86. [261] *Tuché* and *Moira*, accident and predestination.
87. [331]
88. [30]
89. [286]
90. [69] Badly torn fragment.
91. [332]
92. [18]
93. [115-116]
94. [20] This is a larger fragment of 67 (Thief and the night, Thief and the night), a line known in Eustathius before the recovery of a papyrus version. And see Edmonds 46.
95. [72] Both sides of the poem torn away.
96. [90]
97. [289]
98. [91]
99. [78] A fragment with three mutilated words.
100. [23]
101. [104]
102. [298] An Olympic victory chant.
103. [313]
104. [188]
105. [194] A guess, possibly a wild one.
106. [61] A shred of papyrus.
107. [95]
108. [156]
109. [318]
110. [10]
111. [306]
112. [43]
113. [82] The satire was provoked by the superstitious reaction of the people to the solar eclipse of 14 March 711 B.C.
114. [51]
115. [232]
116. [92]
117. [187]
118. [80] This fragment has

also been translated as the opening of 175 [81].
119. [126] A badly torn fragment. The translation is of lines 14-15 only.
120. [52]
121. [1]
122. [41] A ruin of paper, and the translation perhaps neater than called for.
123. [206]
124. [149] The only decipherable word among the remains of five.
125. [199] Scarcely legible, but admitting of conjecture.
126. [124] "Calamitous" is a conjecture. "Wretched," "embattled," something like.
127. [86]
128. [49]
129. [4]
130. [Edmonds 124]
131. [296]
132. [189]
133. [217]
134. [221]
135. [199] Badly torn fragment.
136. [212] Partly conjecture.
137. [71] Fragment torn on both sides.
138. [48] The Greek is simply *frog*. The context would be either a fable or an insult, hence the extension beyond lexicography.
139. [16]
140. [246-247]
141. [125]
142. [54] Restoration by Lasserre.
143. [249.2]
144. [225] The first line is supplied. Plutarch quotes the passage, saying that Fortune is like the woman in Archilochos who carries water in one hand, fire in the other. We don't know what symbolism, if any, Archilochos had in mind.
145. [130] Both sides of the poem torn away.
146. [46] Moeurs asiatiques.
147. [307]
148. [129] Mangled fragment.
149. [320]
150. [287] Field canteen.
151. [174]
152. [135] Only the *ykide* of *Kyrikides* can be read.
153. [94]
154. [68] Line endings only.
155. [200]
156. [208]
157. [231]
158. [182-183] Compare 8.
159. [218]
160. [181]
161. [193] Bonnard translates this: *tu n'as donc pas de coeur au ventre*; Edmonds: *for thou hast no gall to thy liver*. I don't know what it means.
162. [32]
163. [321]
164. [304]
165. [220]
166. [45] The Greek is not as coherent as my English.

Concordance and Notes 101

167. [292]
168. [99] Falstaff at Shrewsbury.
169. [27] Severely mutilated except for two lines. Field hospital.
170. [120]
171. [83]
172. [244]
173. [127] The Greek is not as clear as the translation.
174. [282]
175. [80-81] Only the left-hand half of the fragment exists, and a fair amount of guesswork was needed to stitch the sense together.
176. [251]
177. [28]
178. [140] Mere shred of paper.
179. [322]
180. [50]
181. [141] Badly torn.
182. [131] Shredded and with restorations.
183. [177] Translated by substituting the seven appropriate English words for the seven Greek ones. The alternate version is to suggest what seems to me to be the tone. Aesop derives from Archilochos.
184. [14] Death as a gift again. See 16.
185. [109] Mangled.
186. [21]
187. [280]
188. [70] Badly shredded fragment.

189. [230]
190. [85]
191. [12] Troop ship.
192. [19] From a paraphrase.
193. [284]
194. [56] Shred.
195. [42]
196. [128] Mangled fragment.
197. [224-225, 227-229]
198. [324] A shred of papyrus.
199. [88] The paeon is a hymn either to Apollo or to Asklepios, both gods of healing and of particular importance to soldiers.
200. [333] A spurious fragment.
201. [285]
202. [139] Badly damaged.
203. [98] Much restored. The original, a quotation by Demeas of Paros, seems to have received a shotgun blast.
204. [260]
205. [11]
206. [213] Same as 227 (I knocked him out the door with a vine-stump cudgel). Lasserre emended the old reading *door* to *mountain*. The verb in each means to attack with a cudgel.
207. [312]
208. [310]
209. [236 + 238] The grotesque satire, obviously sexual, in these two fragments has generated some curious explanations. All that's certain is that the meaning is obscene.

210. [145] Badly damaged.
211. [180]
212. [207]
213. [122]
214. [146] Shred.
215. [211] A "black-butted" fellow, literally.
216. [258]
217. [24]
218. [121]
219. [233]
220. [219]
221. [202]
222. [134]
223. [66] Badly damaged.
224. [250]
225. [22]
226. [119]
227. [213] See 206.
228. [74] Two mutilated words, one restored by Lasserre.
229. [293]
230. [147]
231. [117]
232. [89] Neobulé, daughter of Lykambes.
233. [309]
234. [311]
235. [105]
236. [150] Parts of three words on a scrap of papyrus.
237. [197]
238. [4]
239. [47] "Swordsman" I've supplied, since a "son of Ares" would be a soldier.
240. [148] Shredded papyrus.
241. [277]
242. [283]
243. [271]
244. [97] Unless we count a tmesis in the Iliad, this is the first appearance of *panhellenic*.
245. [314]
246. [308]
247. [181]
248. [276] Probably a sexual connotation.
249. [96]
250. [62] Torn on both sides, restorations by Lasserre.
251. [106] Right side missing.
252. [37]
253. [29]
254. [73] A shred of paper.
255. [198] The same as 266. Lasserre translates: *et trancha les nerfs de son membre;* Edmonds, *fracti sunt nervi mentulae.* I give this reading at 266; the reading here was arrived at with aging difficulty and I let it stand.
256. [58] Six letters of the alphabet deployed at random. Restoration of one word by Lasserre.
257. [152]
258. [275] A guess.
259. [79] Shred of paper.
260. [159]
261. [166]
262. [Edmonds 97A, Diehl 80]
263. [167]
264. [163]
265. [175]
266. [198] See 255.
267. [249.1]

Concordance and Notes 103

268. [157] From a paraphrase. Hyperbole in Archilochos, one would think.
269. [84]
270. [161]
271. [67] Shred of papyrus.
272. [102]
273. [235.1]
274. [25]
275. [240-242] Three discrete fragments which fit together neatly.
276. [162] Lucian's paraphrase of an unknown passage in Archilochos. Plutarch also mentions it.
277. [291]
278. [64] Torn on both sides, worse on the left than the right.
279. [2] Possibly an overtranslation. I have extended the image of the sea combed by the wind into what seems to me to be a permissible conceit: nostalgia, loneliness, combing, woman.
280. [281]
281. [288] Birdnest supplied by conjecture.
282. [93]
283. [112]
284. [154]
285. [Edmonds 97B, Diehl 80]
286. [239]
287. [160] Colophon. "You have taken a cricket by the wing," says the Greek, but Lucian in *The Liar* makes the context clear.

www.ingramcontent.com/pod-product-compliance
Lightning Source LLC
Chambersburg PA
CBHW021714230426
43668CB00008B/831